fIRST EPISODE PSYCHOSIS

A GUIDE FOR PEOPLE
WITH PSYCHOSIS AND
THEIR FAMILIES

DONNA CZUCHTA, RN, MSc
KATHRYN RYAN, RN, MSc(N)

camh

Centre for Addiction and Mental Health
Centre de toxicomanie et de santé mentale

A PAN AMERICAN HEALTH ORGANIZATION /
WORLD HEALTH ORGANIZATION COLLABORATING CENTRE

First Episode Psychosis:
A Guide for People with Psychosis and Their Families

Copyright © 1999
Centre for Addiction and Mental Health

ISBN 0-88868-338-3

Printed in Canada

For information on other CAMH publications or to place an order,
please contact:

Publication Services
Tel: 1-800-661-1111 or (416) 595-6059 in Toronto
E-mail: publications@camh.net

Website: www.camh.net

Disponible en français sous le titre
*Le premier épisode psychotique : Guide pour les personnes atteintes
de psychose et leur famille*

CONTENTS

ACKNOWLEDGMENT

This information guide was developed by Donna Czuchta, RN, MSc and Kathryn Ryan, RN, MSc(N) in consultation with the staff of the First Episode Psychosis Clinic and the Clinical Investigation Unit at the Clarke Division of the Centre for Addiction and Mental Health.

We would like to acknowledge Dr. Patrick McGorry and the Early Psychosis Prevention and Intervention Centre in Melbourne, Australia. Our information guide was adapted from psychoeducational material from this centre.

We would also like to acknowledge and thank the following individuals for their support and contributions to the project:

- Monica Bettazzoni, MEd, OT(C)
- Sturla Bruun-Meyer, MD, FRCP(C)
- April Collins, MSW, CSW
- Michael Haswell, BA, RN, RMN
- Shitij Kapur, MD, FRCP(C)
- Beth McCay, RN, PhD
- Helen McGee, RN, BScN
- Wendy Parkinson, OT(C)
- Paul Roy, MD, FRCP(C)
- Carol Speed, MSW, CSW
- Claudia Tindall, MSW, CSW
- Rolando Vasquez, RN, BScN
- Robert Zipursky, MD, FRCP(C)
- and the Nursing Staff, Clinical Investigation Unit.

Finally, we would like to extend our thanks to the patients and families of the Clinical Investigation Unit and the First Episode Psychosis Clinic who assisted us with this project.

INTRODUCTION

This information guide's purpose is to provide information about first episode psychosis, its treatment and recovery. It has been written for people experiencing a first episode of psychosis and their family members, to help them gain a better understanding of this illness. Increased awareness of signs, symptoms and treatment may improve treatment outcomes for people with a first episode of psychosis.

1 WHAT IS PSYCHOSIS?

Psychosis refers to a loss of contact with reality, in which people have trouble distinguishing between what is real and what is not. When this occurs, it is called a psychotic episode.

Psychosis usually first appears in a person's late teens or early twenties. Approximately three out of every 100 people will experience a psychotic episode in their lifetimes. It occurs in men and women and across all cultures and socioeconomic groups.

WHAT IS A FIRST EPISODE OF PSYCHOSIS?

A first episode of psychosis is the first time a person experiences a psychotic episode. A first episode of psychosis is often very frightening, confusing and distressing, particularly because it is an unfamiliar experience. Unfortunately, there are also many negative stereotypes and misconceptions associated with psychosis that may only add to one's distress.

Psychosis is treatable. Many people recover from a first episode of psychosis and never experience another psychotic episode.

2 THE SYMPTOMS OF PSYCHOSIS

Psychosis can come on suddenly or can develop very gradually. There may be early warning signs, such as social withdrawal, or feeling suspicious, anxious, tense, irritable or depressed. Changes in patterns of sleep, memory and thought, and changes in appetite, energy level and concentration, may also occur. Symptoms of psychosis can vary from person to person and may change over time. Some common symptoms are described below.

CHANGES IN THINKING PATTERNS

People experiencing psychosis may have changes in their thinking patterns. For example, they may have difficulty when they try to concentrate, follow a conversation or remember things. Thoughts may become jumbled, or they may not connect in a way that makes sense.

UNUSUAL OR FALSE BELIEFS

People experiencing a psychotic episode often develop false beliefs called delusions. A person may be truly convinced of a belief that is not shared by others, and even the most logical argument cannot change his or her mind. Examples of such beliefs include believing that one is being followed by others, or being monitored by cameras, or believing one's thoughts are being controlled by an outside force.

CHANGES IN PERCEPTION

During psychosis, people may hear, see, smell, taste or feel something that is not actually there. For example, they may hear voices or noises that no one else hears, see things that are not there, or experience unusual physical sensations. These changes in perception are called hallucinations.

CHANGES IN FEELINGS AND MOOD

Mood swings are often experienced during a psychotic episode. A person may feel unusually excited, depressed or anxious. He or she may also feel very little emotion or show less emotion to others who are around.

CHANGES IN BEHAVIOUR

People experiencing a psychotic episode may behave differently from how they usually do. Often the changes in behaviour are associated with the symptoms described above. People may laugh at inappropriate times or become upset for no apparent reason. They may spend more time alone or seem less interested in friends, school or work. The symptoms of the illness may also disrupt sleeping and eating patterns. For example, people may sleep less because they are preoccupied, or they may not eat for fear their food has been poisoned.

Some people experiencing a psychotic episode may feel very depressed, and think that life is not worth living. People experiencing suicidal thoughts may attempt to hurt themselves. Suicidal thoughts should always be discussed with a health professional/therapist. Family members may need support and assistance to cope effectively in such situations. In an urgent situation, take the person to the emergency department of the closest hospital to receive treatment.

Symptoms of psychosis get better with treatment.

3 THE CAUSES OF PSYCHOSIS

In most cases, it is difficult to know what has caused the first episode of psychosis. Current research indicates that a combination of biological factors, including genetic factors, create a situation where a person is vulnerable to, or at a greater risk of, developing psychotic symptoms. A number of brain chemicals, including dopamine and serotonin, may play a role in how psychosis develops. A stressful event may trigger psychotic symptoms in a person who is vulnerable.

In the first episode of psychosis the cause may be particularly unclear. Therefore, it is important for the individual to have a thorough medical assessment, to rule out any physical illness that may be the cause of the psychosis. This assessment involves medical tests as well as a detailed assessment by a mental health professional.

4 THE DIFFERENT TYPES OF PSYCHOSIS

There are a number of mental illnesses that can include psychosis as a symptom. In the early phases of a psychotic episode, it is usually difficult to diagnose the exact type of psychosis that is happening. This is because the factors that determine a specific diagnosis are often unclear during the psychotic episode. It is important to recognize and understand symptoms, and to communicate them to the treatment team. Any concerns or questions about diagnosis should be discussed with a mental health professional.

The following list provides the names and brief descriptions of different types of psychotic illness.

SCHIZOPHRENIA

The term schizophrenia refers to a type of psychosis in which a person experiences some psychotic symptoms for at least six months, with a significant decline in the person's ability to function. The symptoms and length of the illness vary from person to person.

SCHIZOPHRENIFORM DISORDER

This type of psychosis is the same as schizophrenia except that the symptoms have lasted for less than six months. The illness may completely resolve or may persist and progress to other psychiatric diagnoses, such as schizophrenia, bipolar disorder or schizoaffective disorder.

BIPOLAR ILLNESS

With this type of illness the symptoms of psychosis relate more to mood disturbance than to thought disturbance. A person will experience mood elevations (mania) and sometimes depression, which may persist or fluctuate in intensity. When psychotic symptoms arise, they often reflect the person's mood. For example, people who are depressed may hear voices that put them down. People who are experiencing an elevated mood may believe they are special and are capable of doing amazing things.

SCHIZOAFFECTIVE DISORDER

During this type of psychosis, a person will experience symptoms of schizophrenia and symptoms of a mood disturbance, either at the same time or alternating over time.

DEPRESSION WITH PSYCHOTIC FEATURES

Sometimes a person will experience a severe depression with symptoms of psychosis without the mania associated with bipolar disorder. This type of depression is referred to as a psychotic depression or depression with psychotic features.

DRUG-INDUCED PSYCHOSIS

The use of drugs such as marijuana, cocaine, LSD, amphetamines and alcohol can sometimes cause psychotic symptoms to appear. Once the effects of the drugs or alcohol wear off, the symptoms of psychosis will usually resolve. However, the symptoms themselves may require medical treatment.

ORGANIC PSYCHOSIS

Symptoms of psychosis may appear as a result of a physical illness or a head injury. A thorough medical examination should be conducted to rule out or confirm this type of psychosis. This examination may involve some tests or investigations such as a brain scan.

BRIEF PSYCHOTIC DISORDER

Sometimes symptoms of psychosis come on suddenly and, in some cases, are triggered in response to a major stress in the person's life, such as a death in the family. This illness usually lasts less than a month.

DELUSIONAL DISORDER

This type of psychosis consists of very strong and fixed beliefs in things that are not true. Changes in perception, such as hallucinations, are not seen in this illness. A delusional disorder does not usually affect a person's ability to function.

It may be difficult to make a diagnosis in the early stages. Therefore it is not usually helpful to focus on a particular diagnosis. It is also important to remember that everyone's experience of psychosis is different. Course and outcome will vary from person to person.

5 TREATMENTS FOR PSYCHOSIS

Psychosis can be treated, and many people make a good recovery. Research suggests early intervention can lead to a better treatment outcome. Therefore, it is important to get help early. However, in the early stages of psychosis, people often do not know what is happening to them, and do not seek treatment right away. Some people may feel there is nothing wrong or that symptoms will go away on their own. Others, if they are aware of the problem, may have concerns about the required treatment.

ASSESSMENT

Before a specific treatment is recommended, a thorough assessment is completed by mental health professionals, a group that can include psychiatrists, psychiatric nurses, occupational therapists and social workers. In the assessment, you will have an interview with a mental health professional. This will help him or her get an understanding of your experience. Your family, partner and/or friends will also be interviewed to get background information that may help with understanding the context of your symptoms. Blood tests and other investigations, such as brain scans, may be recommended by the psychiatrist to rule out any physical causes of the symptoms.

DIAGNOSIS AND TREATMENT

The information gathered from the interviews and investigations will help the team determine the type of psychosis you are experiencing, its possible causes and the best way of helping you. Treatment may be recommended either on an outpatient basis or in hospital. Treatment usually consists of medication and psychosocial interventions (see below).

MEDICATION

Medication is usually essential in the treatment of psychosis. It relieves symptoms of psychosis and plays a critical role in preventing further episodes of illness.

There are many medications available that help relieve the symptoms of psychosis. Medications used to treat the symptoms of psychosis are referred to as antipsychotic medications, sometimes known as neuroleptics. These medications are generally divided into two categories: typical antipsychotics and the newer atypical antipsychotics.

Typical antipsychotic medications that are commonly used include:
chlorpromazine, flupenthixol, fluphenazine, haloperidol, loxapine, perphenazine, pimozide, thioridazine, thiothixene, trifluoperazine and zuclopenthixol.

Atypical antipsychotic medications include:
clozapine, olanzapine, quetiapine and risperidone.

Current evidence suggests that all these medications are equally effective in treating a first episode of psychosis. They will differ from one another in terms of their side-effects and, as a result, some medications will be better tolerated by some people and other medications will be better tolerated by others.

Treatment begins with a low dose of medication that is monitored closely for any side-effects. These will usually occur within the first hours, days or weeks of starting treatment. If side-effects develop, the physician may prescribe a lower dose, add a medication to reduce the side-effects, or recommend a different medication altogether.

The details of a specific medication program will be worked out with the physician. If the first antipsychotic medication given does not produce satisfactory results, the person with psychosis will usually be given one or two additional trials of the medications listed above. The goal is to use the least amount of medication possible to relieve symptoms, and to keep side-effects to a minimum. Antipsychotic medications are not usually beneficial right away. It may take two to four weeks of treatment to notice significant improvement.

Most side-effects tend to diminish over time. Some people experience no side-effects.

Though they are annoying, side-effects are usually not serious. Common side-effects include: tiredness, dizziness, weight gain, dry mouth, blurry vision, restlessness, stiffness, constipation and muscle spasms.

Atypical medications as a group are less likely to cause restlessness, stiffness and tremor, but are more likely to cause other side-effects such as weight gain.

People who take antipsychotic medication for many months or years risk developing some involuntary movements. This is referred to as "tardive dyskinesia" and usually is evident as unplanned spontaneous movements of the tongue, lips, jaw or fingers. For every year that a person receives antipsychotic medication there is a five per cent chance of developing tardive dyskinesia. This rate adds up over the years of treatment so that after two years the risk is 10 per cent and after five years it is about 25 per cent. If tardive dyskinesia does develop, there are ways to identify it at an early stage and to modify treatment. This will reduce the risk that tardive dyskinesia will persist or intensify. It is hoped that the atypical antipsychotic medications will be less likely to cause tardive dyskinesia, but as yet this has only been established in the case of clozapine.

Clozapine is a medication that has been proven to be effective for people who do not respond well to standard antipsychotic medications. It is not used as a first-line treatment because it carries some special risks, including possible harm to white blood cells. While these risks are low, people who take clozapine need to have weekly blood tests to check their white blood cell count.

It is important to note that medication must be taken even after the symptoms have been relieved. When medication is discontinued too early, there is a very high risk that symptoms will return. This does not necessarily happen right away, and can happen a number of months after medication is stopped. It will be important to talk with your own doctor to know how long you should remain on medication.

PSYCHOSOCIAL INTERVENTIONS

CASE MANAGEMENT

People recovering from a first episode of psychosis often benefit from the services of a case manager or therapist. This person will be a nurse, occupational therapist, psychologist or social worker who has specialized training and experience in psychiatry. A case manager provides emotional support to the person and the family, education about the illness and its management, and practical assistance with day-to-day living. This assistance can help the person re-establish a routine, return to work or school, find suitable housing and obtain financial assistance. Case managers often suggest consultation with other team members for specific concerns. They may also recommend programs in the community that contribute to recovery and provide a stepping-stone to longer term goals involving work or school.

A case manager, or another member of the team with specialized expertise, may provide the following interventions:

SUPPORTIVE PSYCHOTHERAPY

Going through a first episode of psychosis may leave you feeling very frightened, confused, and overwhelmed. Having someone to talk to during the recovery period is an important part of treatment and is critical to the adjustment process. Supportive psychotherapy involves meeting with a case manager or therapist on a regular basis. This support can help you make sense of the illness, address its impact on your self-esteem, and help you to cope and adapt. Supportive psychotherapy aims to help you understand and accept the illness experience and get on with your life.

VOCATIONAL COUNSELLING

People dealing with a first episode of psychosis often need help with a wide variety of work and school problems. You may worry about your ability to pursue work or school, or you may need help with your career options. If this is the case, a referral to an occupational therapist can help. Occupational therapy explores your objectives and interests. Skill-oriented evaluations are used to identify what your strengths and challenges are in a work or school setting. To help you make a successful transition back to school or work, you can also receive short-term counselling and be linked to resources in the community.

6 FAMILY INVOLVEMENT — ISSUES AND CONCERNS

Many partners and families find the onset of psychosis extremely distressing and feel helpless and confused. Their involvement is important in the overall plan toward recovery.

Family members can learn about the nature of the illness, and available treatment options, by working with the treatment team. Family members can provide information about the person's symptoms, how they developed, and how the person functioned before the illness. Throughout treatment, families can receive support and education during sessions with the treatment team. Family members can also receive guidance on issues such as how to relate to, and support, a relative who is ill. For example, it is best to communicate in a calm, clear manner, and to avoid overwhelming the ill relative with too much information. It is also important for family members to be aware that their relatives need time to recover and may not be able to fully engage in all activities of daily living right away. A structured approach to gradually taking on tasks and activities usually works best.

Many families find that they need to develop coping strategies and effective communication skills to help them support the ill family member. Individual family counselling, psychoeducation workshops and support groups can help develop these strategies and skills. They can also provide ongoing emotional and practical support, as well as education about the illness. It is important that family members find a balance between supporting their recovering relative and finding time for themselves. This helps them prevent exhaustion and avoid becoming "burned out."

7 THE PROCESS OF RECOVERY

People dealing with a first episode of psychosis should be actively involved in their own treatment and recovery. This can be achieved by learning about the illness and its treatment, and the ways to prevent further illness episodes. The recovery process will be more successful if the person learns to recognize warning signs or symptoms, learns how to manage stress, builds up a social support network, and engages in valued activities, such as work, school or leisure.

A FINAL WORD ABOUT RECOVERY

The course of recovery from a first episode of psychosis varies from person to person. Sometimes symptoms go away quickly and people are able to resume a normal life right away. For others, it may take several weeks or months to recover, and they may need support over a longer period of time.

Psychosis is treatable and many people will make an excellent recovery.